Vishnu

Subhadra Sen Gupta has written over thirty books for children. Right now she is waiting for a time machine so that she can travel to the past and join Emperor Akbar for lunch. She loves to travel, flirt with cats and chat with autorickshaw drivers. If you want to discuss anything under the sun with her, email her at subhadrasg@gmail.com

Tapas Guha has been working for more than twenty years as an illustrator. He loves to draw comics and illustrate children's books. Ruskin Bond is one of his favourite authors and he loves Tintin comics.

Vishnu

SUBHADRA SEN GUPTA

Illustrated by
TAPAS GUHA

RED TURTLE
RUPA

Published in Red Turtle by
Rupa Publications India Pvt. Ltd 2017
7/16, Ansari Road, Daryaganj
New Delhi 110002

Sales centres:
Allahabad Bengaluru Chennai
Hyderabad Jaipur Kathmandu
Kolkata Mumbai

Text copyright © Subhadra Sen Gupta 2017

Illustration copyright © Tapas Guha 2017

All rights reserved.
No part of this publication may be reproduced, transmitted,
or stored in a retrieval system, in any form or by any means,
electronic, mechanical, photocopying, recording or otherwise,
without the prior permission of the publisher.

ISBN: 978-81-291-4737-0

First impression 2017

10 9 8 7 6 5 4 3 2 1

The moral right of the author has been asserted.

Printed at Nutech Print Services, New Delhi

This book is sold subject to the condition that it shall not,
by way of trade or otherwise, be lent, resold, hired out,
or otherwise circulated, without the publisher's prior consent,
in any form of binding or cover other than that in which it is published.

Contents

How Do You Fool an Asura? / 7

The Sea of Milk / 22

Just Three Steps / 36

HOW DO YOU FOOL AN ASURA?

Everyone knows that Lord Vishnu is a kind and generous god. It is not only people who pray to him for help, even other gods call out to him when they are in trouble. They know that Lord Vishnu will come up with a clever plan and he will never let them down. Even Lord Shiva, the powerful god of destruction, was once in such a pickle that only Vishnu could save him.

It all began with an asura called Bhasmasura and the old story of the fight between the devas and the asuras. In the heaven, Swarga, lived the devas and devis or the gods and goddesses. Below was the earth and under that was the netherworld of Patala. Here lived the asuras who were the enemy of the devas and they were always fighting with each other. The asuras were powerful fighters who possessed magical powers and they were always trying to find ways to throw the devas out of Swarga. So the devas had to be ready for battle all the time.

A new danger appeared for the devas with an asura named Bhasmasura and there is an interesting story behind his name. This asura wanted to defeat the devas but he knew that the gods were great warriors. So he needed some special fighting powers. No asura could give him such power, so he came up with a very clever idea. He would ask a god for it!

You may wonder, why would a god help an asura? Well, there was this rule that if anyone prayed very hard to a god like Brahma, Vishnu or Shiva, the god had to listen. So if anyone—even an asura or rakshasa—prayed to a god, then the god had to answer the prayers. This asura decided he would pray to Shiva because he knew that Shiva loved his devotees and usually listened to their prayers.

So he went into a forest, sat down under a tree and began to pray, 'Oh Lord Shiva, please, please answer my prayers.'

The asura prayed and prayed. Nothing happened.

Shiva was meditating in a cave on Mount Kailash, high in the Himalayas, and he did not even hear the asura. So the asura prayed louder and harder. Months passed but there was no reply from Shiva.

Then the asura tried new ways of praying. He stood on one leg and prayed. He raised one arm to the sky and prayed. He sat under the searing hot summer sun and prayed. He stood in the snow and prayed. When it rained he was drenched but he did not stop praying.

He just went on and on and on...

Finally the asura's voice got so loud, it echoed across the land, floated up to Mount Kailash and Shiva opened his eyes and thought, 'What was that? Is someone praying to me? Hmm... I'd better go and talk to this devotee of mine.'

Shiva stood up, slipped his feet into his wooden chappals, picked up his begging bowl and his trishul trident, and then he flew down from the Himalayas with his bull Nandi and landed before the asura. The moment he saw Shiva, the asura promptly fell at his feet.

'Ah!' said Shiva as he looked at the asura in surprise and said thoughtfully, 'So you were praying to me. Your prayers were so loud it disturbed my meditation.'

'I am sorry about that, my lord,' the asura mumbled apologetically, 'but this was an urgent matter.'

'Urgent is it? Fine! How can I help you?'

'My lord, I have a small request to you...'

'Ah, a request! So what's new?' Shiva sighed. 'People always pray to me because they want something. So my friend asura, what do you want?'

'My lord... oh wonderful deva...' the asura was smiling away in this very oily way, 'I just want to become immortal, please Lord...'

'Eh?' Shiva frowned in surprise. 'Immortal as in living forever?'

'Yes my lord.' The asura's smile got even wider. 'I don't want to die. So no one should be able to kill me.'

Shiva glared angrily at the asura. 'Now I understand! Your plan is to live forever and attack and kill the devas. And you are asking me, a deva, to help you? Are you out of your mind, you stupid asura?' Shiva

picked up his trishul and turned to go. 'Never!'

'Umm...' the asura looked a bit apologetic and then said, 'Okay, maybe not immortality but...'

'But WHAT?' Shiva yelled, quite furious.

'You did promise you'll answer my prayer.'

'Yes I did, but remember, immortality is not possible. In a battle you die. If you fall ill, you can die. Everyone dies. That is the way of the world.'

'But *you* live forever,' the asura grumbled.

'I am Shiva! I am a great god, you fool! If we, the gods, were not there, how would creation go on?'

The asura shrugged, 'Then can I ask for a different boon instead? Remember, you promised!' Shiva nodded gloomily, knowing that he could not refuse. 'Then my lord, I want the power to turn anyone into ashes just by touching him or her on the head.'

Shiva thought for a while and then said, 'Fine! You can have the power. If you touch anyone on the head, he will be burnt to ashes.'

The asura thanked Shiva and walked away with a huge grin on his face.

Ashes are called bhasma in Sanskrit and that is how the asura's name became Bhasmasura.

Soon Bhasmasura went quite crazy as he began killing anyone he did not like. He would rush up and touch them on their head and they would turn to ashes. People, asuras and even devas began to run away from him. The asuras made him their king and he led the asura army to fight the gods.

During the battle, as long as the devas fought him from a distance using spears, bows and arrows, they were safe. The moment Bhasmasura got close, he would rush in, touch the deva warrior on the head and poof! The poor warrior was turned into a pile of ashes.

Lord Indra, the commander-in-chief of the army of the devas, was a very worried god as his soldiers were becoming very nervous of fighting the asuras. When he discovered that Bhasmasura had got this power because of a boon from Shiva, he went to Lord Vishnu and begged that Vishnu should help.

So Vishnu rushed to Mount Kailash where he found Shiva and his wife Parvati sitting in their cave.

'How could you do this, my lord?' Vishnu asked Shiva. 'How could you help an asura when you are the supreme deva of all devas?'

'Very true, Lord Vishnu,' Devi Parvati nodded,

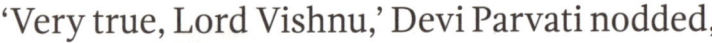

'I have been asking him the same question.'

'Well, you two should know that the asura first wanted the boon of immortality. Then no deva would have been able to kill him.'

'Oh! Then what did you do?'

'I refused, of course!' Shiva turned his prayer beads with a grim smile, 'But I had to give him something. He had been praying to me for years and I had promised him a boon.'

'That was very clever,' Vishnu sighed. 'But I am worried that this will get you into trouble. Why don't you take the boon back?'

'I can't! A boon is forever.' Shiva did not really believe Vishnu needed to worry, and it looked like he could not help by taking the boon back.

As he got up to leave, Vishnu said to Shiva, 'My lord, if you get into trouble with Bhasmasura, call me immediately. Only I can help you.'

Meanwhile Bhasmasura was enjoying himself. Everyone was so scared, they obeyed all his orders and gave him whatever he wanted.

A huge palace to live in? One was soon built for him by the asuras.

Lots of gold jewellery and silk clothes? The devas sent him a gift hamper.

A feast of delicious dishes to eat? The best chefs of Swarga were sent to work in his kitchen.

But asuras have one problem. They are easily excited and soon all this power went to Bhasmasura's head. He thought he could get everything.

One day he saw Devi Parvati as she was picking flowers in the Swarga garden. 'Who is that beautiful woman picking flowers?' Bhasmasura asked a servant. 'Now that I am the king of the asuras, I need a queen. I think I'll marry her.'

'You can't sire!' the servant protested. 'That is Devi Parvati and she is Lord Shiva's wife!'

'Hah! And I'm the great Bhasmasura!' He boasted, 'I'll make Shiva run away and then I'll marry her.'

So Bhasmasura went to Shiva and told him he wanted to marry Parvati. When an angry Shiva refused, Bhasmasura decided that the only way he could marry Parvati was to turn Shiva into ashes. As he came rushing towards Shiva, the god realized what was happening and he began to run and Bhasmasura came right behind him, with his arm stretched, trying to touch Shiva's head.

'HELP!' yelled Shiva. 'Vishnu, come quickly! I am in serious trouble!'

Vishnu, who had been watching the scene from afar, had to come up with a plan very quickly. Luckily he had a special power and could change his shape. Vishnu closed his eyes and instantly turned into a beautiful woman called Mohini.

Vishnu-Mohini flew in and landed in front of Bhasmasura. The moment he saw the pretty woman, Bhasmasura forgot all about chasing Shiva and stopped in his tracks.

'Oh! Another beautiful woman!' he cried in delight. 'And she is prettier than Parvati.'

'Who are you?' he asked her.

'I am Mohini,' said Vishnu-Mohini, fluttering her lovely eyelashes and giving a teasing smile. 'And who are you?'

'I am Bhasmasura, the king of the asuras. Will you marry me, Mohini, and become my queen?'

Mohini looked thoughtful and then said, 'I will do so if you can prove to me that you really are a powerful asura.'

'What do I have to do, pretty girl?' Bhasmasura gave an evil grin.

'Can you dance?' asked Mohini.

'Of course I can dance!' Bhasmasura puffed up his chest. 'As I am the most powerful asura, I have to be the best dancer in the world.'

'Maybe...' Mohini looked doubtful. 'But can you dance better than me?'

'Yes I can.' Then Bhasmasura had a brainwave. 'Why don't we have a dance contest and see who dances better?'

'Fine!' said Mohini. 'I'll dance first and you have to follow me and dance in exactly the same manner.'

'That's easy!' Bhasmasura boasted. 'Go ahead!'

So Mohini began to dance and Bhasmasura watched her carefully and copied her movements.

Mohini twirled on her toes and Bhasmasura did the same. She waved her arms like a flying bird and he followed. She stamped her feet and bent at the waist and he just grinned and did the same. Then Mohini began to dance faster, twirling and twisting, bowing and stamping, as her feet moved like lightning. Then her fingers began to move in complicated mudras.

As Mohini danced faster and faster, Bhasmasura began to pant as he had to watch her very carefully

and keep following. He was so busy watching Mohini, he forgot everything except the dance moves.

Then as she twirled away, Mohini raised her hand and touched her head and Bhasmasura did the same. And POOF!

Bhasmasura had turned into ashes!

Vishnu laughed as he changed from Mohini and turned back into his handsome god-like self. Then the magnificent god turned to Shiva and said, 'So my lord, Bhasmasura is a pile of ashes and your troubles are now over!'

Shiva bowed. 'Thank you, my lord Vishnu. It was a brilliant plan. You really are the cleverest of the devas.'

'Ah yes, so I am!' said Lord Vishnu with a smile.

THE SEA OF MILK

A long, long time ago, there was a sage named Rishi Durvasha who spent his time in prayers and meditation. He was a wise and clever man but there was one problem with him. If Durvasha got angry, he would become so furious that it made the earth shake and everyone ran away to hide behind trees.

An angry Durvasha would let terrible curses fly, and remember, when a rishi curses, it always comes true.

So everyone was very careful about what they said or did around Durvasha. Who knew what would make him angry? Unfortunately, Lord Indra forgot this and my, did he get into trouble!

One day Indra was riding an elephant through the forest and he came upon the thatched hut where Durvasha lived. The rishi was sitting before the holy yagya fire, busy chanting mantras, and Indra decided to meet him. He sat down beside Durvasha and joined in the prayers.

Durvasha was very happy and after the yagya was over he said, 'My lord Indra, I am very pleased that you joined my yagya and as a symbol of my gratitude, here is something for you.'

Durvasha picked up a beautiful garland of pink lotus blossoms and, as Indra bowed, he put it around Indra's neck.

Now Indra was a very proud god. Coming out of the hut he thought, 'What will I do with this garland of lotus blossoms? I am the great Indra, the powerful commander-in-chief of the army of the gods. I don't wear flowers around my neck. I wear only gold and jewels.'

Indra's elephant was standing nearby munching some banana leaves. Indra took off the lotus garland and draped it around the elephant's head. The elephant grabbed the garland with its trunk and happily tore it into shreds.

Durvasha, who was standing at the door of his hut, saw all this and felt very insulted. He thought, 'I gave the garland to Indra as a gift and he put it on that elephant! How dare he!'

Durvasha's face began to turn redder and redder as his eyes grew round with rage and then he let the curses fly.

'I curse you Indra!!' he yelled. 'You think you are so powerful that you can insult a rishi like me? I curse that you and your deva army will lose all your powers as fighters and you will lose Swarga.'

Hearing the shouts Indra stopped at once and ran back to fall at Durvasha's feet, begging for forgiveness. But Durvasha refused to listen to him.

Soon enough the curse began to come true. The gods or devas who lived in Swarga were always fighting their enemies—the asuras who wanted to conquer Swarga. Now when King Bali, the ruler of the asuras, heard of the curse, he was delighted! His army of asuras came marching in and a war started. The devas were getting weaker and weaker and ran away from the battlefield to save their lives.

Indra was a very worried god as it seemed that the devas would soon be thrown out of their heaven unless something was

done to remove Durvasha's terrible curse. Indra needed help and who could he go to except Lord Vishnu, the kindest and most generous of the gods.

Indra travelled to Vaikunth where Vishnu lived and fell at his feet, mumbling, 'Help me... oh my lord Vishnu... please help me!'

Vishnu listened to Indra's story and frowned, 'You made Rishi Durvasha angry? That was foolish of you!'

'Durvasha likes you,' Indra said hopefully. 'Perhaps if you spoke to him he'll listen to you and take back his curse.'

'Impossible! You know perfectly well that rishis do not take back either blessings or curses. That is the rule.' Vishnu scratched his chin thoughtfully, 'We have to find another solution. Let me think...'

As Indra sat and watched, the great god paced up and down his palace, thinking very hard. 'There is only one way. We have to find the Amrita Kumbha—the pot containing the nectar of immortality...'

'What will that do?' Indra asked puzzled.

'When the devas drink the nectar they will become immortal. Then they cannot be defeated in battle as they will live forever.'

'Oh! What a clever idea!' Indra sprang up in excitement. 'Tell me, where is that pot of nectar kept? I have to get it immediately.'

'Well, that is the problem. The Amrita Kumbha lies at the bottom of the Sea of Milk and it won't be easy to find.'

'Oh, that is no problem at all!' Indra said excitedly. 'I can get Lord Varuna to dive down and get it. After all, he is the god of the oceans and he is a champion swimmer.'

'Varuna won't be able to dive so deep. We have to churn the sea so that the pot rises to the surface.'

'Churn a sea?' Indra looked amazed. 'But for that we'll need a huge stick and a very long rope.'

'We could use the mountain called Mandara as a stick and Vasuki, the giant snake, as a rope.'

'Fine!' said Indra happily. 'Let's go to work then.'

'Not so fast!' said Vishnu. 'This is a very difficult job and you'll need help. Mandara is a very heavy mountain and you'll have to drag it to the sea. The devas no longer have the strength to do it. Then the churning will also need a lot of strength and you will need help.'

'Help?' Indra frowned. 'Whose help?'

'The asuras.'

'The asuras?' Indra stared at Vishnu in shock. 'They are our enemies. Why would they help us?'

Vishnu smiled. 'They would help if you promise to share the amrita with them. The asuras want to be immortal too.'

'Are you joking?' Indra yelled going all red with anger. 'If the asuras also get the amrita, how can we defeat them in the battlefield?'

'Calm down. I have a plan... Once the pot of nectar has been found, I will make sure that the asuras do not get it. Trust me, only the devas will drink the nectar of immortality.'

Indra was not very happy but he obeyed as Vishnu was his only hope. So he wandered into the court of King Bali, the ruler of the asuras. Bali was a great king and even though he was a bit surprised, he welcomed Indra and listened to his request. As Vishnu had predicted, the asuras agreed to help the devas to churn the Sea of Milk, hoping to get a share of the amrita. Bali was sure that the asuras would grab the pot first as they were stronger.

So, to everyone's surprise, the devas and the asuras decided to work together. They dragged Mandara to the Sea of Milk. Then they wrapped the snake Vasuki around it. The devas held Vasuki's tail and the asuras held his head. Then they began to pull, making Mandara whirl and churn the sea until the water was foaming and frothing, with waves rising higher and higher.

All this pulling and churning led to a new problem. Mandara was very heavy and it began to crack the earth until everyone feared that the bottom of the sea would break into many pieces. Seeing this, Vishnu turned himself into a giant tortoise called Kurma Avatar and dived down. He placed himself under Mandara in his tortoise form and became a pivot for the mountain so that the churning could go on.

With all the churning, poor Vasuki the snake was having a very difficult time. He was being pulled so hard, it hurt him and the poison that was inside him now began to pour out of his mouth. Everyone feared that the poison would kill all living creatures. At Vishnu's suggestion, all the devas and asuras

began to pray to Lord Shiva to come and save them.

Shiva came and quickly drank the poison. It was so strong that it turned his neck blue. That is why one of the names of Shiva is Neelkantha or the blue-necked god. The churning went on and soon many magical things began to appear from the bottom of the Sea of Milk.

First appeared Surabhi, the cow of plenty, who gave you whatever you asked for. She is also called Kamdhenu.

Then appeared the beautiful goddess Varuni carrying a pot of wine, and the asuras who liked drinking wine welcomed her.

Then a tree called Parijata floated up and when it was planted in Swarga by Indra, its flowers filled the air with its heady perfume.

Chandra, the moon god, was plucked from the water by Shiva who placed it on top of his wild coils of hair.

A beautiful goddess appeared next, sitting on a lotus. This was Lakshmi, the goddess of wealth. All the asuras fell in love with her but she went and sat with Vishnu, as she was his beloved wife.

Rambha, the pretty celestial dancer or apsara, came next.

She was followed by Uchhaisravas, the magical horse which was taken by the asuras.

Then Airavat, the white elephant, appeared and he was taken by Indra.

A brilliant jewel called Kaustabha floated up and was picked up by Vishnu, who wore it on his neck.

The jewel was followed by Shankha, a sacred conch shell, and Dhanush, a magical bow.

Finally, a handsome rishi named Dhanvantri appeared on the surface of the sea. He was the guru of Ayurveda, the ancient science of medicine. Everyone saw with amazement and excitement that Dhanvantri was carrying the Amrita Kumbha, the pot that held the nectar of immortality.

Immediately the devas and asuras began to fight. The asuras being stronger because of Durvasha's curse, managed to capture the Amrita Kumbha.

'What is happening, my lord Vishnu?' wailed Indra. 'Do something! You promised, remember?'

'Of course I remember! Do not fear!' said Vishnu and quickly changed shape again. Now he became a madly beautiful woman named Mohini.

Vishnu as Mohini walked around the asuras with a lovely smile and her beauty was so dazzling that all the asuras forgot about drinking the amrita. Instead they began to argue with each other angrily about who would marry Mohini.

While the asuras were busy fighting, Mohini quickly changed back into Vishnu, picked up the Amrita Kumbha and began to run. Just then Vishnu's vehicle, the half-eagle half-man called Garuda, came flying down from the sky and Vishnu sprang on Garuda's back and flew away.

The asuras could not fly and so they stood there and yelled and screamed in anger. Vishnu flew right across the land and high up over the mountains of the Himalayas and straight into Swarga, the heaven of the devas.

Soon the devas arrived in Swarga and drank the amrita. Now their powers came flooding back. So when they fought the asuras again, the devas won the battle and all the asuras ran away.

'Hey, Lord Indra!' said Vishnu, 'I kept my promise, didn't I?'

'Yes you did, my lord Vishnu, and thank you,' said Indra. 'You truly are the kindest, cleverest and greatest among the gods.'

JUST THREE STEPS

Lord Brahma, the god of creation, created a universe of three worlds. First there is Swarga or heaven where the gods and goddesses, along with the devas and devis live with the celestial musicians called gandharvas, and beautiful dancers called apsaras.

Then there is our earth, or Prithvi, where men, women, children, animals, birds and fish live.

Finally there is the world below the earth called Patala where the asuras live. The asuras are great fighters like the devas but they are rather bad tempered, easily excited and full of pride.

In many of our mythological stories you will read about the devas and asuras fighting with each other because the asuras want to conquer Swarga and throw out the devas. That is because Patala is a dark and gloomy place and the asuras looking up at Swarga think, 'What a lovely place Swarga is! It is full of light, and hills, forests and lakes abound. We want to live there!'

Long, long ago, the asuras used to live on earth. Now how did they end up in Patala? The story takes us to another avatar of Lord Vishnu.

You have read about the churning of the Sea of Milk, and how the asuras had helped the devas to get the Amrita Kumbha, the pot of nectar of immortality. The ruler of the asuras, King Bali, had agreed to help the devas because they had promised to share the amrita with the asuras.

However, Vishnu had tricked the asuras and escaped with the amrita. Once the amrita was drunk by the devas they became powerful again and promptly defeated the asuras.

So King Bali was a very angry asura. He decided to hold a huge religious ceremony called a yagya and invited many priests to the ceremony. He planned to get the priests to bless him so that the asuras became powerful once again.

On the day of the yagya a huge fire was lit, dozens of priests sat around it chanting mantras at the top of their voices as they threw flowers and sandalwood into the fire. Then they dipped big ladles into pots of fragrant ghee and poured the ghee to make the fire glow brighter and brighter.

Soon the yagya magic began.

A golden chariot with four white horses to draw it appeared from the fire.

Then came many weapons and armour—a sword with razor sharp edges, a gold-plated bow and two magical quivers that would always be full of sharp iron-tipped arrows.

Finally, Bali was gifted with magical armour—a chest plate that no arrow or sword could ever pierce.

Indra was watching it all from Swarga and he began to get worried. With all these mighty weapons Bali would be invincible. So he went to the sage Rishi Kashyapa and said, 'O great Guru, the devas are in danger again as King Bali is getting chariots and weapons from the yagya. What do we do?'

'I cannot help you, my lord,' Rishi Kashyapa shook his head. 'You should go and ask for Lord Vishnu's help. He is the cleverest amongst us all and he is sure to have a plan.'

Indra looked a bit doubtful, 'Do you think he'll help us again? What if he says no? Then we are in real trouble.'

Kashyapa's wife Aditi was listening to them and she said, 'I will pray to Vishnu. He is a kind and generous god, and I'm sure he won't refuse me.'

Aditi prayed to Vishnu with all her might and the god was so pleased that he decided to be born as her son. To everyone's surprise, Aditi's child was very short, a dwarf, and so he was called Vamana. This was the fifth avatar of Vishnu.

Vamana now hurried to the place where Bali was holding the yagya. He looked like a poor Brahmin priest. He wore a cotton dhoti, carried a begging bowl and an umbrella. All priests were welcome at the yagya and he was taken into the palace. Bali was a great king, so all the guests were offered the finest food and drinks, silk dhotis, saris and shawls.

Then Bali made an announcement: 'I am very happy with the results of the yagya and I want to give gifts to all the priests here. Ask for anything you want—gold or land, jewels, horses or elephants and I will give it to you. No one will be refused.'

One by one the priests spoke of what they wanted. One man asked for a village, a second begged for gold and another wanted a bag of coins. Finally, little Vamana walked up to Bali.

'What can I give you, sir?' Bali smiled kindly at the small figure standing before him.

'I am a simple man, Your Majesty,' Vamana said, 'I don't need much. Give me land just the length of three steps.'

Bali frowned, 'I'm afraid I don't understand you. What do you mean by "three steps"?'

'I want the land,' Vamana explained patiently, 'that I can cover when I take three steps.'

Everyone began to laugh as Bali smiled down at Vamana. Was this Brahmin joking, Bali wondered. How much land could he cover in just three steps

when he was so short?

Bali waved a hand, 'Of course you can get the land! Please take the three steps.'

Then as everyone watched in amazement, an extraordinary thing happened. Right before their eyes, the tiny Vamana began to grow bigger and bigger and bigger... Soon he was so tall that his head touched the sky!

The giant Vamana Avatar now took his first step and it was so huge, it covered the sky!

Then Vamana Avatar took the second step and it went across the whole of the earth!

Then he looked down at Bali and asked, 'You gave me the gift of three steps but the sky and the earth have already been covered. Where do I step next?'

Bali, who now realized that Vamana was in fact Lord Vishnu, kneeled at the god's feet and said, 'Step on my head, my lord.'

So Vishnu-Vamana stepped on Bali's head and the asura king was pushed down below the earth into the netherworld of Patala. Since he was their king, all the asuras followed him down to Patala. And there King Bali rules forever.

Of course the asuras still come up from Patala and head for Swarga to fight the devas often. There are many interesting stories about the devas and the asuras since this fight never ends!

THE AVATARS OF VISHNU

It is said that whenever the world is in trouble, Vishnu appears on earth. He comes in many shapes and forms. These are called avatars.

There are ten avatars of Vishnu:

1. Matsya, the fish
2. Kurma, the tortoise
3. Varaha, the boar
4. Narasimha, the man-lion
5. Vamana, the dwarf
6. Parashuram, Rama with an axe
7. Rama, the prince of Ayodhya
8. Krishna, the king of Dwarka
9. Gautama Buddha, the teacher
10. Kalki, the avatar who is yet to come

KUMBH MELA

While Vishnu was flying towards Swarga with the Amrita Kumbha, four drops of amrita fell on the land at Allahabad, Haridwar, Ujjain and Nashik. Every year huge gatherings called Kumbh Mela are held in these places.

BALI ON EARTH

There is a beautiful town by the sea named Mahabalipuram in Tamil Nadu. Many lovely stone temples stand on the beach here. It is said that this is the place where King Bali was pushed down to Patala. People in Kerala believe that their land was once the kingdom of Bali and once a year he comes up from Patala to see his people. They celebrate the festival of Onam to welcome him back for a few days.